Puzzle Island

Dear Friend,

I am in urgent need of your help.
You must travel at once to Puzzle Island.
Take this map as your guide. Go to my treehouse.
Your next instructions are written in the diary
which you will find there. Keep the map in the diary.

I dare not write more. If news of my discovery falls
into the wrong hands, it could spell disaster.

Do not delay!

Yours puzzlingly,

Ambrose Fogarty

July 18th, 1890

Welcome to Puzzle Island! I knew I could count on you!

Recently, I discovered a pair of creatures from a species
believed to have been extinct since the late 17th century.
How they survived and how they came to be here, I can only guess.
But in the interests of conservation, I have decided to return them
to their original habitat. My aim is to establish a breeding colony
there, so that this rare species will survive, after all.

There is, however, a problem. There is only room for one
of these remarkable creatures in my hot-air balloon.

Even as you read these words, I will be flying to a secret location
with the male specimen. Its mate remains safely hidden here
on Puzzle Island. I rely on you to find her and bring her to me.

I expect you are wondering how you can find something
without knowing its identity. Well, you must discover what it is
and where it is for yourself, by solving a puzzle I have devised.

My last few weeks before leaving the island will be spent preparing
clues that can only be solved by someone who really loves animals.
So, if anyone else should visit the island and find my diary,
the identity and whereabouts of the female will remain a mystery.

On the opposite page, you will see a painting of the treehouse.
Four well-known animals are hidden in it. See if you can find them.

If you have difficulty, look carefully at the frame.
The names of the hidden animals can be found
by re-arranging the letters missing from each alphabet.
Once you have the names, move on to the next page.
Take my diary and the map to the Beach of Shady Palms.

July 27th, 1890

Well done, my dear Friend. You are already one step nearer to finding the mysterious inhabitant of Puzzle Island.

Finding the hidden creatures will be good practice for you. You will need to know all their names, if you ever hope to discover my secret!

This is the Beach of Shady Palms.

If the coconuts are ripe, try persuading a monkey to climb up a palm tree and fetch you one. I can think of nothing more delightful than sitting in the sun and listening to the waves, while sipping delicious cool coconut milk.

When I painted this picture, the coconuts were not yet in season, so the monkeys were nowhere to be seen. Again, there are four creatures hidden in this picture. You must find them and work out their names, before you can explore Puzzle Island any further.

Perhaps, the parrots will be able to help you. They are always around, whatever the time of year. But do not listen to their idle chatter for too long, or you will be misled!

When you are ready, turn to the next page of my diary, and walk southwest, until you reach the Rainbow Waterfall.

Beach of Shady Palms

August 5th, 1890

Never in all my travels have I seen a more breathtaking view
than Rainbow Waterfall. The crashing and roaring
of the water is almost deafening. What a contrast
to the gentle lapping of the waves along the seashore!

If you have followed my directions, you should be standing
on the eastern side of a deep ravine overlooking the falls.
If you are hungry, you may enjoy a few bananas. But be warned,
they only grow on the other side of the ravine.

I would have to be very hungry indeed, before I would risk
the perilous rope-swing across. And don't expect the monkeys
to help you. I have never known a monkey who was willing
to share a banana!

When I painted this picture, a herd of elephants was walking
towards their water-hole for an early morning bath.
You will meet them again later, but first you must continue
with the puzzle.

Once more, four creatures are hidden in my painting for you
to spot. I expect you are getting good at finding them.
But from now on, their names will become longer and harder.

When you are ready, turn to the next page of my diary.
Walk south, along the edge of the ravine, to the Volcano.
But watch your step! Those mischievous monkeys leave
their banana skins in some very dangerous places!

August 17th, 1890

As you near the volcano, you will begin to observe
a startling change in the landscape. The last eruption
left a trail of devastation. Cooled, hardened lava covers
the ground. Charred, blackened trees stand like skeletons
and the pungent stench of sulphur fills the air.

Do not be alarmed, my good Friend! It is quite safe
for you to pass through, as long as the volcano lies
dormant and all is peaceful.

It was not so safe, though, when I painted this dramatic picture
of the last fiery eruption. Even though it was midnight,
the shooting flames lit the island like day.
The heat was so intense that the paints almost dried
before I could apply them to the canvas!

It was dangerous indeed, and very foolish of me to sit
at my easel, as the red hot lava crept closer.
But to complete my puzzle, a picture of the volcano was a must.

The overwhelming heat had another, much stranger effect.
All over the island, flowers began to bloom, and buds opened
on the trees. By morning, my painting was complete
and the air seemed to be filled with butterflies,
dancing from blossom to blossom to gather nectar.

As you have probably already guessed, there are
four more animals for you to find in this picture.
When you have spotted them and worked out
their names, turn to the next page of my diary.
Walk west along the cliff top
to Lightning Tree Canyon.

August 20th, 1890

The weather on Puzzle Island is almost always perfect.
But once every few years, a terrifying tropical storm
leaves chaos in its wake. One year, there was a sandstorm
in the desert. Another year, a gigantic tidal wave carried
a vast whale onto the beach and left him stranded.

Exactly when lightning struck the old tree that stands
at the mouth of the canyon I shall never know.
For as long as I have been visiting the island,
it has always looked the same, stunted and totally devoid of life,
except for the parakeets that roost in the branches.

I could only work at my canvas early in the morning,
for as soon as the sun was at its height, the heat was
so intense that the mountains appeared to shimmer.

Early morning was also the safest time to paint.
Lightning Tree Canyon is simply crawling with snakes.
Being cold-blooded, they are inclined to be sluggish, until
they have basked for some time in a warm patch of sunlight.
Then they are deadly and move like quicksilver.

So, my friend, do not linger. Find the four hidden animals
and their names as soon as possible. Hurry north, through
the centre of the canyon. Then turn to the northwest and
keep going until you reach the gate of the Garden of Statues.
You may now turn to the next page of my diary.

August 31st, 1890

Step into the Garden of Statues, where time and almost
everything else seem to stand still. The only sounds
you will hear are the eery cries of the peacock and his mate.

They are the only creatures I have ever seen enter this strange place.
Perhaps most animals are wary of the uncanny silence.
Or maybe the peacock, who behaves like the king of the island,
chases everyone else out of his palace garden.

How the statues got here, I cannot say. I like to imagine
that they were sculpted by some ancient civilisation.
Or that they were on board a galleon, that ran aground
on the coral reef, laden with marble and onyx carvings
from the east. Perhaps, some poor shipwrecked sailors
dragged them ashore and cultivated the garden, to remind them
of the home they would never see again.

When I painted this picture, summer was almost over.
Petals were falling from the huge sunflowers and the peahen
pecked at the dry brown seed heads. I completed it only just
in time. As I made the last few brush strokes, the peacock
shook his splendid tail and two iridescent feathers fluttered
to the ground. In a few weeks' time, he would have moulted
every single one, ready to grow a new set for the spring.

When you have found the four creatures hidden in this picture
and worked out their names, you may turn over
to the next page. Then, walk out through the gate and head
in a northeasterly direction towards
the Deadly Desert.

Garden of Statues

September 8th, 1890

You are about to cross the Deadly Desert. There will be
danger at every step, so make sure you are wearing a stout
pair of shoes and are carrying an adequate supply of water.

The snakes are not so numerous as in Lightning Tree Canyon.
But they are more than made up for by an abundance
of tarantulas and scorpions. Their venom is just as fatal
and they are much harder to spot.

Normally, the desert is a dull, dry place, hardly worth
a visit. But when I painted this picture, there had been
a freak autumnal cloudburst, causing many of the cacti
to blossom in the space of a few short hours.

Once again, there are four more creatures for you to find
in this picture. But they are getting harder to locate,
aren't they? And their names are longer and more awkward
to decipher. You must know them all, before turning
to the next page of my diary.

To cross the Deadly Desert safely, walk north in a perfectly
straight line. Watch where you tread and keep sipping
your water. The vultures are hovering. They are longing
for you to make a mistake.

If you survive, keep heading north and climb
the steep, grassy slope immediately ahead.
If you hear a loud snoring noise,
there is no need for alarm.
You are about to enter the Cave of Dreams.

THE DEADLY DESERT

I hope, for your sake, that the great bear is sleeping
as soundly at this moment, as he was when I painted
his portrait. For, if he is awake, he will never allow you
to pass through the cobweb curtain into his cave.

The atmosphere in the Cave of Dreams can most accurately
be described as soporific. The moment I stepped
into its cool and restful interior, the desire to sleep
almost overwhelmed me. Bats dozed restlessly
between the stalactites, and even the robin,
who had intended to sing, yawned prodigiously instead.
How easy it would have been to be lulled into a false sense
of security and allow my eyelids to close.

So, my friend, do not sleep like the others, but stay awake
and keep your wits about you. It is time to search
for the next four hidden animals. Do not forget,
you can work out their names from the letters missing
from the alphabets surrounding the picture.

Once you have completed your task, tiptoe to the back
of the cave, and follow the narrow rocky passage through
the heart of the mountain. At times, the tunnel will become
so small, that you may have to crawl on your hands and knees.
But it is worth the effort. Once you have reached the mouth
of the tunnel, you may turn to the next page of my diary.

Your next step will be a step back in time.
You are about to enter the Forgotten Valley.

Apart from myself, I suspect that you are the only human
being to set foot in this remarkable spot. Surrounded
on three sides by steep cliffs, and cut off from the rest
of the island by a chain of impassable mountains, the Forgotten
Valley has remained unchanged since the beginning of time.

Do not be alarmed by what you see. I have explored
this fascinating place many, many times,
and contrary to popular belief, I have found dinosaurs to be docile
and peaceful creatures, who would not intentionally harm you.

How thrilling it is, to see with one's own eyes, creatures
that we have known only through ancient fossilised remains.
It is amazing how familiar many of them look, thanks to
the artists' impressions we so often see in books.

There are other creatures and plants here, that are beyond
the imagination. The endless variety of insect life defies description.
I have spent many hours sketching them in detail.
I am sure that you will want to return and explore
more thoroughly. This could be the very place
to locate the mystery creature I have asked you to find.

First, however, complete the puzzle. In my painting of
the Forgotten Valley are four more animals to find.
Don't forget to check their names. You will need to know
them, later on!

When you are ready, creep back through the Cave of Dreams,
turn left, and walk down to the Lily Pond.
You may now turn to the next page of my diary.

October 1st, 1890

Welcome to the Lily Pond, one of the most charming
and tranquil places imaginable. It feels good to be back
on the warmer side of the island. Here it is like
perpetual spring, no matter what time of year.

No paint could possibly capture the vivid pink of the lilies,
but I hope I have managed to portray how these seemingly
still waters positively teem with life.

Only once before have I seen lily pads of such remarkable size.
That was during one of my expeditions to the islands
of Hawaii. This particular species of lily has pads
that can grow to the size of a cartwheel. They are quite capable
of supporting the weight of a small child.

Many is the time I have envied the amazing lily-trotter,
with her elongated toes, hopping from pad to pad
with effortless ease. If I could do the same,
the short cut across the pond would take many hours
off my journey back to the treehouse.

You, too, must walk the long way round. But only after
you have found the four hidden animals and deciphered
their names. When you are ready, turn right, and walk
along the bank of the pond, until you reach the western edge
of the ravine by Rainbow Waterfall. Here, at last,
you will be able to pick the bananas
you missed earlier, if there are still any left!

Then, walk down the steep stone steps,
cut into the rocky sides of the cliff face,
and eventually you will come
to the Elephant's Waterhole.

You may now turn to the next page of my diary:

Lily Pond

October 6th, 1890

Well, my Friend, your journey and the puzzle are both almost at an end. I expect you are hot and tired and longing for a cool refreshing shower.

If the elephants are there, I am sure they will oblige. There is nothing they like better than squirting each other with trunkfuls of water. I have joined in their bathtime capers many times myself after a long day's exploration.

Elephants are among my favourite animals. Despite their huge size and tremendous strength, they are gentle and loving. We can learn so much from them and must do all we can to preserve them.

This is probably the friendliest place on the island. There are no harmful or dangerous creatures for miles around.

Painting this picture took far longer than any of the others, because my curious companions were continually pushing their long dripping trunks into my paints and canvas. Even so, it was hard to be cross for long, especially when I heard the infectious laughter of the parrots.

Look with care. These are the last four hidden creatures you will have to discover. I suppose you are finding them easily now, but their names are more difficult to work out.

Did you manage to find ALL the hidden animals and their names? If not, you must turn back and look again. Without them, the last stage of the puzzle will remain a complete mystery! Once you are ready, turn to the last page of my diary and solve the final parts of the puzzle.

At last, you are ready to find the whereabouts of my mystery creature.
But first you must discover what it is.

Take a pencil and paper and write down the names of all the animals
you have found, together with the symbols in the corners of the page they are in.

The first letter of each animal's name will replace one of the symbols
in the following message. The symbols will help you decide
which letter goes where.

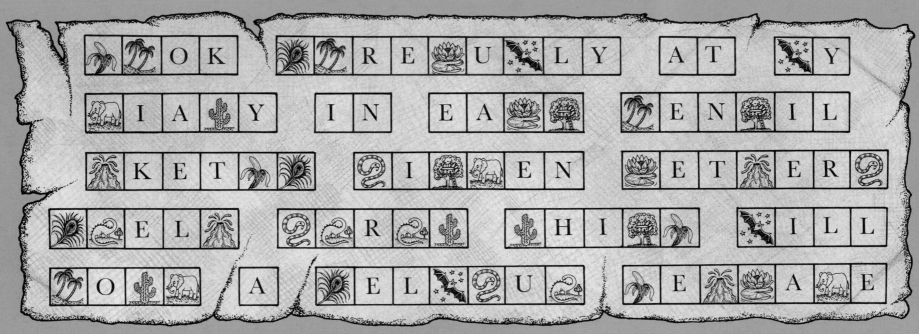

If you understood the message, carry out the instructions and you will finally know
WHAT you are looking for.   Congratulations!

Now, can you spot WHERE it is hidden? It is not under cover!

If you need help, solve this coded message.

X PB WXSSTC DC IWT UGDCI RDKTG DU IWT QDDZ.
XU NDJ RPCCDI UXCS BT, ADDZ XC IWT QDGSTG UDG
IWT ATIITGH IWPI HETAA BN CPBT. YDXC IWT ATIITGH
IWPI BPIRW, UGDB IWT RTCIGT DU TPRW HFJPGT.
BN TNT HWDJAS QT LWTGT IWT ILD AXCTH RGDHH.

As you know, the creature's name is spelt with only two different letters.
These two letters are the key to the code.

Down the left hand side of your paper, write out the alphabet, starting
with the first letter of the creature's name. (For example, if it starts
with 'D', write D-E-F-G and so on, until you get to Z. Then continue
down the paper, from A onwards, until the alphabet is complete).

Now, write the second letter of the creature's name, on the top line,
next to the first letter of its name. Then, once again,
continue the alphabet to Z and complete it by starting again at A.

This gives you a code in which the letters on the left represent those
on the right. Done it? You are now ready to decode the message.

Where do you have to take the female specimen to?
There's one more message, with a poetic clue!